MY HERO IS A DUKE...OF HAZZARD

Billie Jean Williams Edition

Billie Jean Williams

My name is Billie Jean Lowe Williams. I am from Bear Creek North Carolina and I'm a mother of 4 kids and 2 angels in heaven.

It was 1979 and I was four years old. One night this one

show came in tv and I saw a car chase and my dad and I

were curious about it. It was called The Dukes Of Hazzard.

 From then on I was completely hooked on The Dukes Of

Hazzard. My dad and I watched it every week. Every Friday

night I was glued to the TV with my daddy sitting right

beside me watching with me.

 I enjoyed watching the show so much my mama signed me

up for the Dukes Of Hazzard fan club and any time we would afford it I had to have something from the show. I went to school with my metal Dukes of Hazzard lunch box, wearing my Dukes shirt, eating my meals on my Dukes TV tray.

Then one Saturday morning, a cartoon on.. The Dukes of Hazzard Cartoon. It came on TV and I would get up every Saturday morning just to watch the cartoon then go back to bed.

John Schneider

Dec 11, 2020 · 🌍

Get a copy today at: www.johnschneiderstudios.com #photolab

Mama and Daddy thought it was funny how I would just wake up on a weekend just to watch that one show and go back to sleep. The Dukes Of Hazzard wasn't just a show, it was a show that taught family always sticks together. That family is number one. It taught morals and values and you can't get any of that out of a TV show today.

 To me The Dukes Of Hazzard cast was more then just characters in a show they were like family. Uncle Jesse reminded me of my daddy. Cooter reminded me of my

cousin that worked at his garage, and my daddy helped him

alot.

Photo credit: Billie Jean Williams with Marshall Thornhill's General Lee.

I grew up going to the garage all the time. I just never found my Bo or Luke. I used to have a dreams of me being in the General Lee with Bo and Luke. I even had a big plastic General Lee that I used to try an get it up on two wheels.

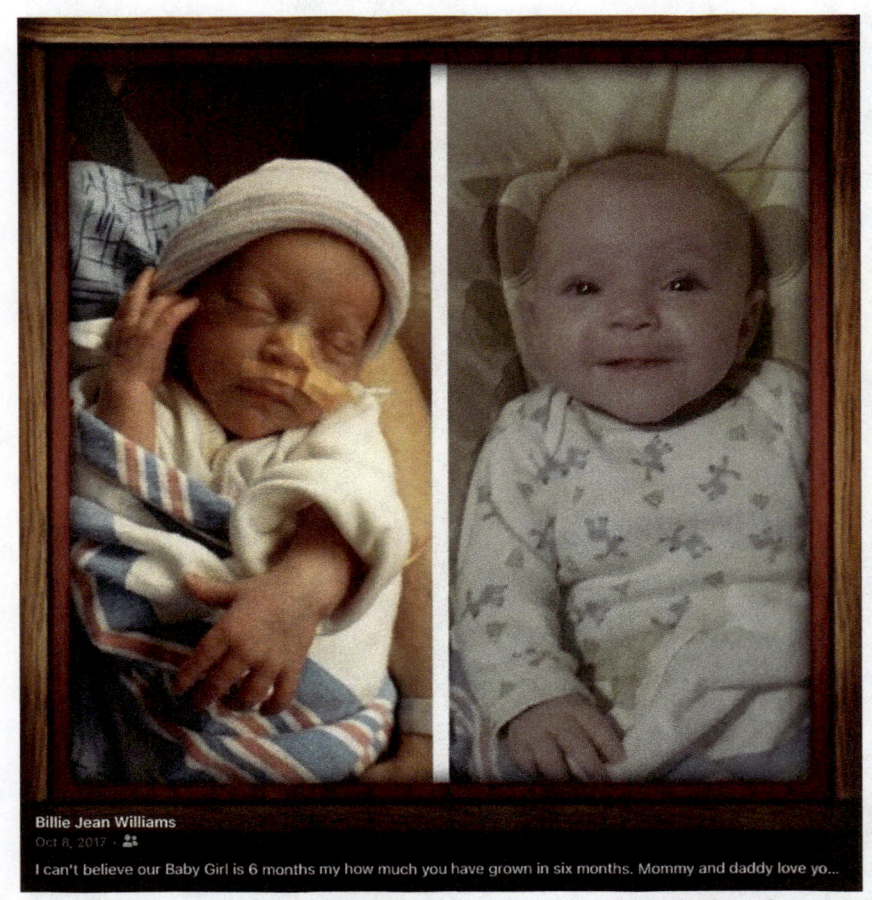

One day in when I pushed it just right and when it hit the wall it popped up on two wheels and rolled down the side.

When it went on the two wheels i was so happy. I finally got it.

I was really upset when the show stopped airing on TV.

 **John Schneider** is with **Alicia Allain** at **DUO**.

May 14 · Rantoul, IL · 🌐

Love the food here!!! John Schneider fans 👀

In 1996 my first son was born and whenever we were at the stores and either saw the Dukes of Hazzard on vhs or anything that was Dukes of Hazzard, we got it. My son grew up watching the show even though we only had a few episodes on vhs, we would watch them alot.

Linda Williams
Mar 16, 2016 · 👥
With Billie Jean Williams.

He had a little tikes car that was orange and wanted us to put 01 on the side and the flag on top. So I did just like he asked. I even wrote General Lee of the top also. He would crawl in it threw the window, never opening the door .

Micheal would even climb in and out of my daddy's truck

threw the window all the time. He also wanted to try the

hood slide. One day I did my best to help him slide across

the hood and he was smiling from ear to ear. My daddy and I

bought him a remote control General Lee one year for

Christmas. He use to jump that car over anything and

everything he could.

Photo credit: Billie Jean Williams

In 2002 I had a still born little girl and in 2004, I was lucky to

have my second son. He was a twin and I lost his twin while I was two months pregnant. Luckily, Mitchell survived.

Also that year our house burned down and all my childhood memories and my Dukes of memorabilia did also..

One day I saw the Dukes Of Hazzard seasons on DVD in Walmart and I had to have them, so I would get a season every month. I wanted to make sure he grew up watching a show that had morals and values and taught family sticks together just like I did and Micheal.

So Mitchell would watch The Dukes Of Hazzard with me and Micheal a lot. There was even times he would fall asleep watching the show on dvd. Now both my boys would be able to watch the greatest shows ever. Micheal was even able to watch shows he had never seen because we couldn't find my episodes on vhs but I did on DVD. I got all the episodes I could but was missing two. Unfortunately they quit selling

Billie Jean Williams at Birdsong Drive-In

the dvds and I knew I couldn't afford to order them from Amazon or ebay so I waited till I was able to find them and could afford them.

John Schneider
May 15 · 🌐

Look what's almost finished! Let's get dirty! Dirt track that is!!!

My boys and I started to rebuild our collection of Dukes stuff. We had gotten small cars, big cars that played the Dixie horn, models metal cars, even a remote control car. We weren't able to afford to get both boys the remote control General Lee, so we got that for Micheal and another

Billie Jean Williams
Mar 12, 2013 · 🌐
With Micheal Lowe.

General Lee car for Mitchell. I tried to make sure that both my boys had there own cars and Dukes stuff when I was able to afford it. Mitchell would ride in Michael's little tikes car and he would try his best to imitate the Dixie horn .

Photo credit: Billie Jean Williams

Now forty something years later, the Dukes of Hazzard is still my all time favorite show, along with my boys all time favorite show.

In 2017 I had a little girl and went threw hell and back right after I was hospitalized for her first two months of life. I almost didn't survive. It has been an up hill process since then but its well worth it. My kids are my world and I would do anything for them.

John Schneider
Apr 19 · 🌐

I love me some Cameo!

Personalized videos from your favorite celebrities

cameo

V.CAMEO.COM
Cameo - Text me this Cameo!

I wanted to make sure my daughter had the same opportunity that my boys and I did by watching a show with family morals and values so I started putting the Dukes dvds on and she fell in love with the show just like my boys and I did. When she got a little tikes car "What do you think she did? She would crawl in threw the window and it would

Billie Jean Williams

remind me of Micheal an Mitchell all over again.

So Micheal did for her what I did for him he put 01 on the side and drew the flag on top for her and she loved it.

Thanks to my husband, I was able to go to Cooters Place to visit and was able to find and afford the two seasons on DVD

Billie Jean Williams at Birdsong Drive-In

of the Dukes of Hazzard that I didn't have. I was able to find the cartoon and had to have it also.

My daughter got her first General Lee there. Yes, it was cloth car w plastic pellets in it, but its her first one and she slept with it every night.

Photo credit; Billie Jean Williams

One day I met on line, a very nice guy name Sean Gaffey and he has helped me get my Dukes Collection. I built it back up since our house fire in 2004. Now its bigger then it was before. Threw the years I have been able to collect little cars, big cars, pictures, coloring books, scrapbooks TV guides, a cup, shirts and even a Bo duke figurine. I also purchased a great book Sean made with photos from the show.

Since my daddy passed away in 201, I have been collecting more pictures of Uncle Jesse because my daddy wore overalls at one time and a red hat, then moved to red suspenders and his red hat. Uncle Jesse always has reminded me of my daddy.

Photo credit: Billie Jean Williams

I never thought I would ever get to meet John Schneider or Tom Wopat or even Catherine Bach but my dream came true. I have met John Schneider twice now and he is so nice and kind (not to mention he still looks good after all this time). I have been able to actually afford a cd of John Schneider songs and I even have three of his movies on DVD

and can't wait for Poker Run.

My kids loves the Dukes of Hazzard and every chance we get we watch episodes. There isn't another show these days that teach family vales and morals and is safe for children to watch and not have to worry about if there seeing or learning anything bad. The Dukes of Hazzard is a show that is the safest and most enjoyable show to let you kids watch.

Photo credit:Billie Jean Williams

Pamela Anderson Bates

Pamela Anderson Bates
Jun 4 ·

Had to do something to my hair still beautiful ♥️

I been watching Dukes of Hazzard since I was like about 9 or 10 but my son, he's artistic he's just 12 and he love the shows.

Photo credit: Pamela Anderson Bates

Mikayla Faith McDonald

I will make people smile, but inspire many more!

Mendie Davis-Mcdonald

Mikayla Faith McDonald

Photo credit: Mikayla Faith McDonald

Kevins General

Kevins General

Kevins General at Home

Kevins General at Hoyt Lake in Delaware Park

Get well soon Joe!

Hazzard Garage

Photo credit: Michael and Darrell Locket with Marshall Thornhill's Lee.

David Jesse Duke

David Jesse Duke
May 9

Happy Mother's Day Linda from Uncle Jesse.

David Jesse Duke
Mar 14 ·

I hope this book brings joy to Dukes of Hazzard fans and the memories of Denver Pyle.

David Jesse Duke

David Jesse Duke
Nov 18, 2020 · 👥

My youngest Daughter...I think she loves me!

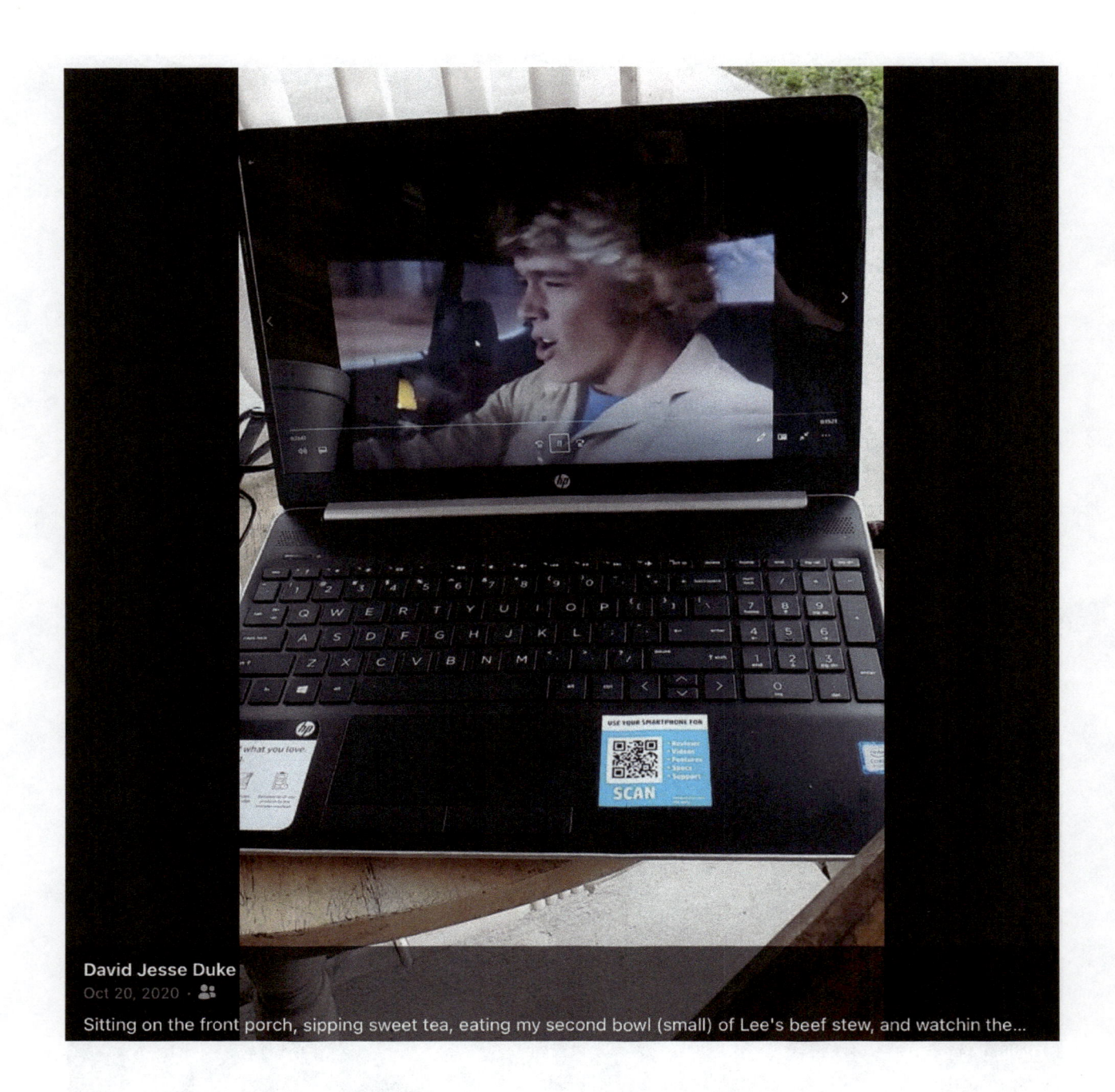

David Jesse Duke
Oct 20, 2020 · 👥

Sitting on the front porch, sipping sweet tea, eating my second bowl (small) of Lee's beef stew, and watchin the...

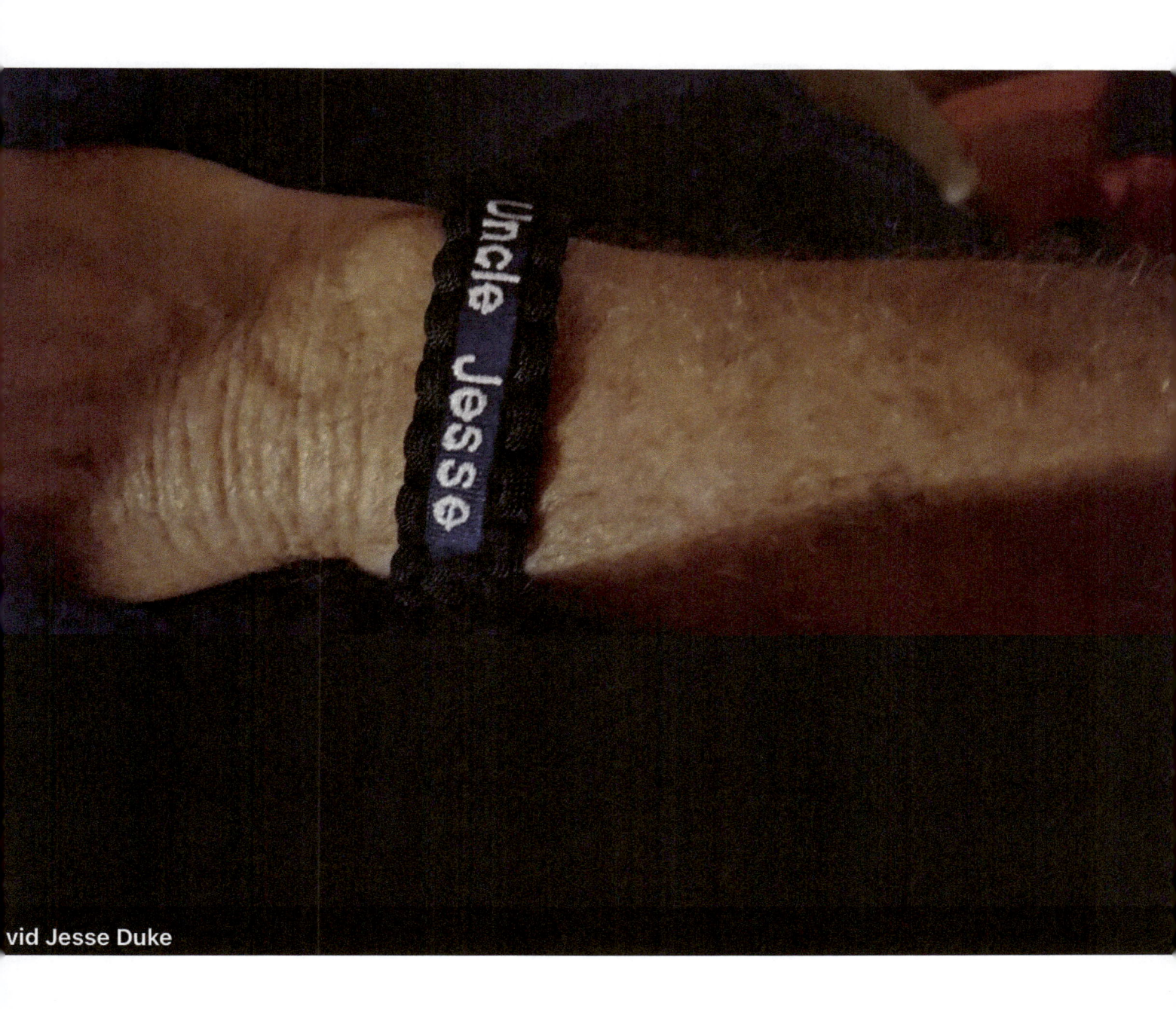

vid Jesse Duke

David Jesse Duke
Oct 10, 2020 · 👥

So excited about going to Cooter's in Pigeon Forge tomorrow that I can't sleep. Shepherd out

Bradley Harrison

Bradley Harrison

Feb 14, 2019 · 👥

With **Gloria Harrison**.

Bradley Harrison
Aug 30, 2019 · 👥

i enjoyed talking to this man and listen to some of his stories and a wonderful person i am glad i got to spend so...

Bradley Harrison
Oct 12, 2019 · 👥

With **Rusty Kash**.

dley Harrison

18, 2019 · 👥

h Tom Sarmento and Gloria Harrison.

Photo credit: Bradley Harrison

"I got the this car 13 years ago and now we are redoing it. It was rebuilt once when I purchased it from a father and son. They built it together and showed it In a some local car show in Missouri. I bought it and brought it back to Kentucky. After my first wife died the car set for the last 8 years up until now.

 The car is going back to original condition, what it was when it was new. My wife and I have bought another Charger and we are making it a General Lee because the car has some history.

 This car came from our good friend Tom Sarmento, he was going to build this car to be a jump car for Corey Eubanks to use at on of the Hazzard Fest for a jump but they never did."

-Bradley Harrison

Rusty Kash (Rusty Cash)

I enjoy making people laugh I enjoy going to the ocean

This is my family my children and my wife there's a picture

there of my grandmother I was 22.

Photo credit: Rusty Cash

Photo credit: Rusty Cash

Photo credit: Rusty Cash

Photo credit: Rusty Cash

Photo credit: Rusty Cash

Photo credit: Rusty Cash

Photo credit: Rusty Cash

Join us in our group this June!

Let's work up a sweat with fun workouts,
...odies to thrive through the hot
... and find more joy in
...re and wellness!

Sherri Schroeder Dell

I'm a homeschool mom, a Scout mom, a g'ma, and a Ret. Army wife.

Sherri Schroeder Dell

Katie Nicole
Apr 15, 2014

With **Sherri Schroeder Dell**.

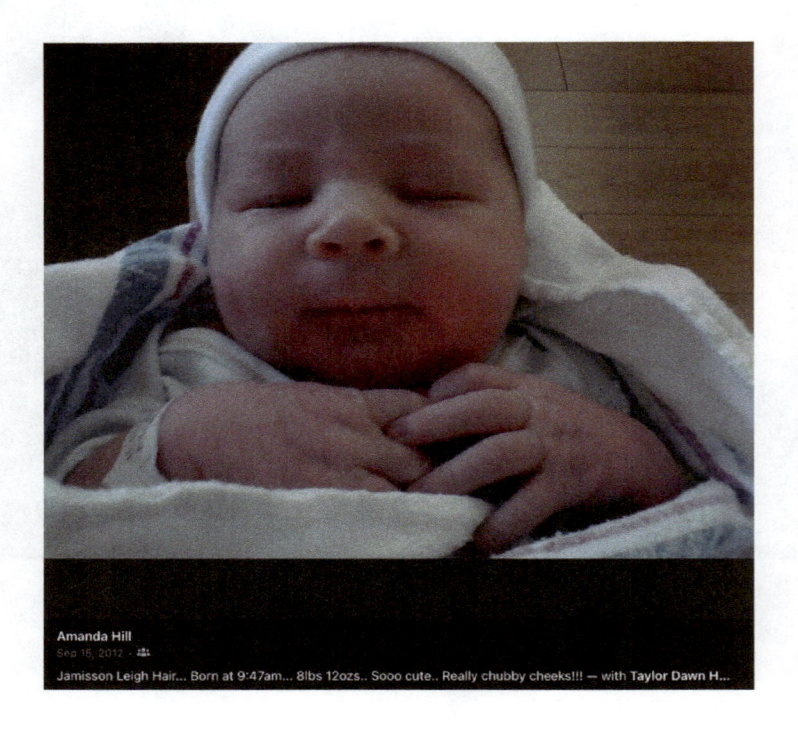

Amanda Hill
Sep 15, 2012

Jamisson Leigh Hair... Born at 9:47am... 8lbs 12ozs.. Sooo cute.. Really chubby cheeks!!! — with Taylor Dawn H...

Amanda Hill

Scott Plaufcan

Photo credit: Scott Plaufcan

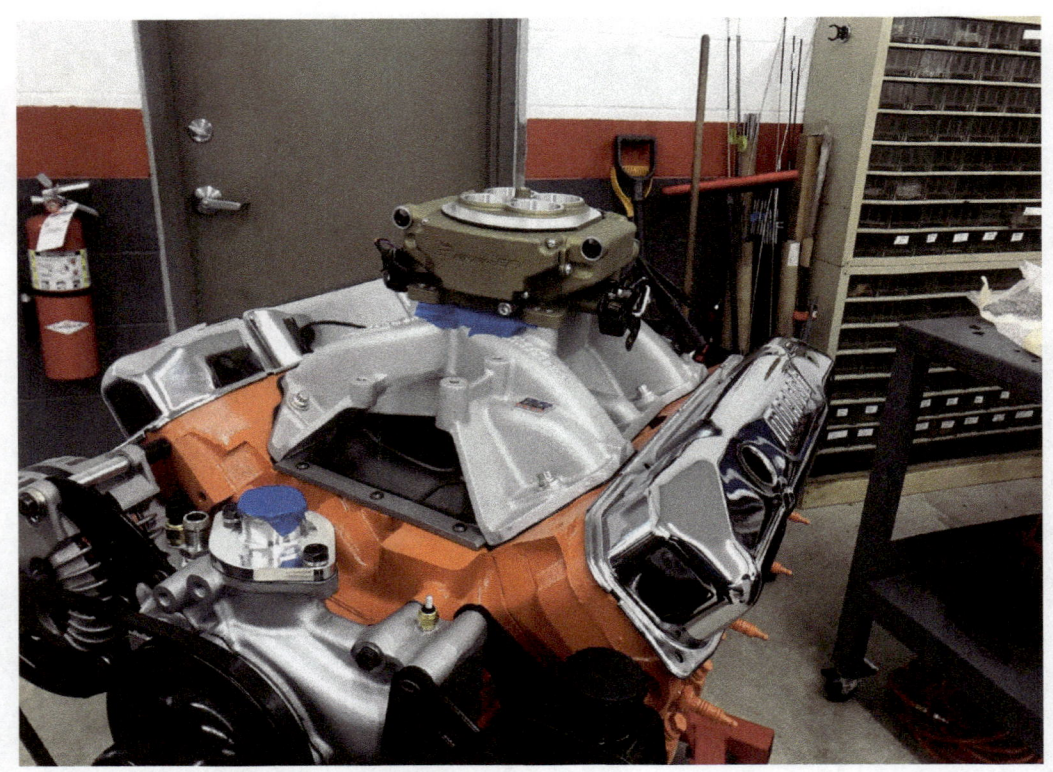

Photo credit: Scott Plaufcan

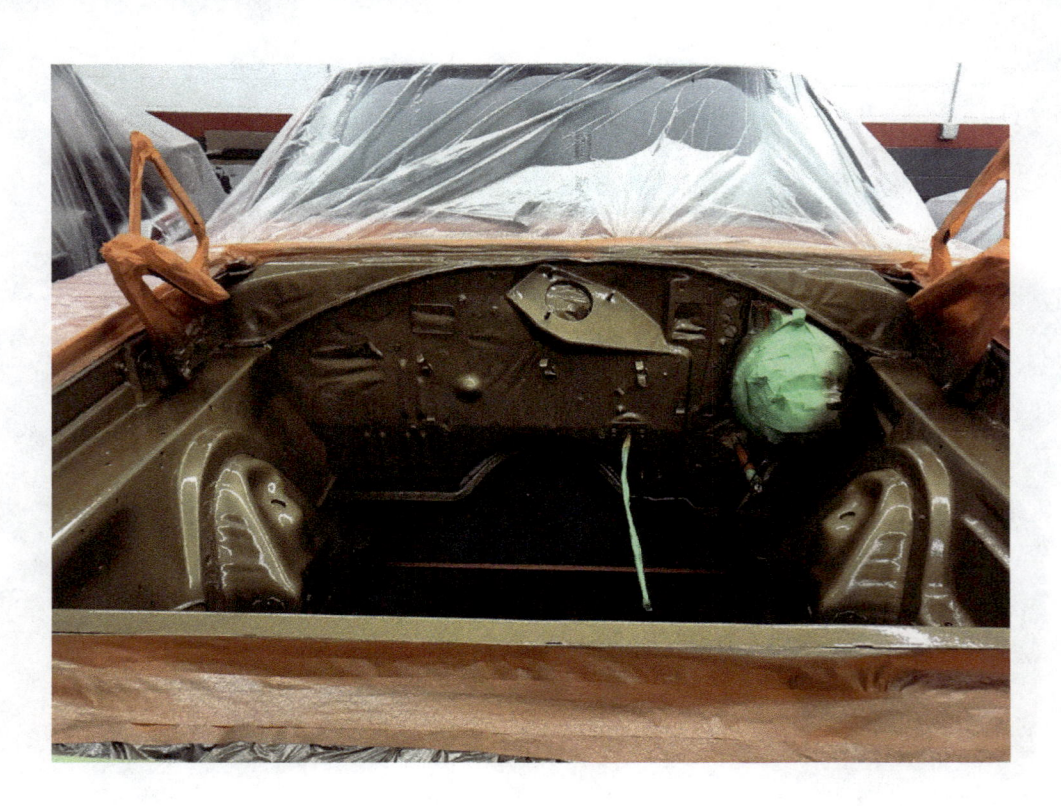

Photo credit: Scott Plaufcan

Photo credit: Scott Plaufcan

Stephanie Stein

I'm an athlete for Special Olympics for 10 years Swimming
Snowshoeing Bowling Bocce I love life!

Stephanie Stein

Photo credit: Stephanie Stein

"Family, that's what the Dukes of Hazzard are all about.

Coming together in any situation to support one anther."

Log on to: Johnschneiderstudios.com

CPSIA information can be obtained
at www.ICGtesting.com
Printed in the USA
LVHW050246200721
693167LV00007B/301

9 781105 494512